WHERE THE STORY OF OUR CITY BEGAN

In AD 1080, Robert Curthose, the eldest son of William the Conqueror 'laid the foundation of a castle whereby the town of Newcastle did afterwards take both her beginning and her name' (SPEED).

However the 'New Castle' wasn't the first stronghold built here to defend the river crossing; a Roman fort, Pons Aelius, stood on the site 500 years earlier. Curthose's wooden castle lasted less than a hundred years before it was rebuilt in stone. This included the Keep, which still casts an imposing presence over the River Tyne.

Newcastle has developed into a bustling modern city, meaning we are incredibly fortunate to have the Keep and the Black Gate survive for people to be able to visit and enjoy. Today, the Castle is popular with locals and tourists alike, who can climb to the rooftop and marvel at the unbeatable views over the regional capital.

Throughout this book, lesser known words are formatted in **bold**. Please refer to the glossary on page 30 for definitions.

© The Heart of the City Partnership, 2017. Nothing may be reproduced in whole or part without the written permission of the publisher. This book may not be sold except by authorised dealers.

Lead Writer/Editor:
Peter Cumiskey

Other writers:
John Nolan, David Silk

Contributors:
Allisdair Bowman, Corey Lyddon-Hayes, Cathryn Howard, Ruth Small

Graphic Design:
David McClure at Velcrobelly.co.uk

Archive images used with kind permission of Newcastle Libraries and Tyne Bridge Publishing. Illustrations by Kelvin Wilson (p. 2, 4 & 6), Judith Dobie (p.5), Geoff Laws (p.7), Caroline Jamfrey (p.9) and Mat Edwards (back cover).

Photographs by Ben Smith, Graeme Peacock, Chris Shieber and Alan Wallace.

This book uses, as its basis, *The Castle of Newcastle upon Tyne* by Barbara Harbottle © Society of Antiquaries of Newcastle upon Tyne, 1977, and the subsequent revisions by John Nolan.

Every effort has been made to provide accurate information. We apologise for any innacuracies, which we would be pleased to correct in any new edition of this guidebook.

A HISTORY OF THE CASTLE

PONS AELIUS: ROMAN 'NEWCASTLE'

In Roman times a road from the south reached the Tyne at Gateshead; following their occupation of Britain in AD 43, they established a settlement at that strategic location. A bridge (*pons* in Latin) was built across the river where the gorge was narrowest. The bridge was named Pons Aelius – 'Hadrian's Bridge' – *Aelius* being the family name of the Emperor Hadrian, who established Hadrian's Wall as the longest-lasting northern boundary of the empire.

Two altars which once stood on the bridge were found in the Tyne in 1903, and are today held at the Great North Museum: Hancock. A replica of one, dedicated to Neptune – god of waters, rivers and seas – is displayed near the Keep.

To guard the northern bridgehead, a fort was established on the hilltop above the river, where the Castle now stands. The fort, also called Pons Aelius was rebuilt by Emperor Severus in about AD 200. It is not known whether the fort was attached to Hadrian's Wall or lay a little to the south. The fort wall may have been irregular in outline, following the edge of the hilltop, but its internal streets and buildings seem to have followed the pattern of other forts.

Nothing is now visible on the surface, but the outlines of the Headquarters Building, Commanding Officer's House, and two granaries, are marked with cobbles to the north and west of the Keep.

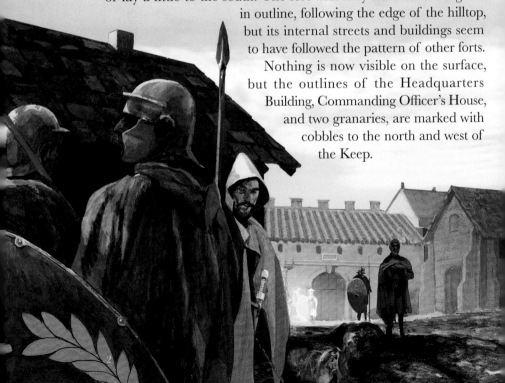

ANGLO-SAXON

Little is known of Newcastle following the fall of the Western Roman Empire, but archaeological evidence suggests that the fort of Pons Aelius was robbed for building materials.

According to some later chroniclers Newcastle had been a monastic settlement called Monkchester – the 'town or city of the monks' – but no evidence has been found to support this claim.

During the construction of the railway viaduct in the 1840s, large quantities of human bone were uncovered. These were assumed to date from the plague of the 1630s. However, archaeological excavations north and west of the Keep between 1977 and 1992 located 660 burials of men, women and children, and many bones from disturbed graves. These ranged in date from the late 600s to the 1200s, showing that the site of the Roman fort had been re-used as a cemetery over a long period. Some of the later graves had stone markers, which are today displayed under one of the railway arches.

North of the Keep, the foundations of a building, thought to be part of a late Saxon church, are visible. This building continued eastwards, overlying the remains of a smaller structure, possibly an earlier chapel.

Below: Pons Aelius.

NORMAN

Following the Norman Conquest in AD 1066, William the Conqueror (1066-1087) was faced with bringing the north of England under control. William Walcher was made Bishop of Durham and Earl of Northumberland. When one of Walcher's knights murdered a Saxon nobleman, the locals rebelled and Walcher was killed in May 1080 at St Mary's Church in Gateshead.

William's retaliation was brutal and the North was laid waste. Later the same year, William's son, Robert Curthose, was campaigning in Scotland. Upon returning he built the 'New Castle' as a way of controlling the river crossing and intimidating the rebellious locals. The site was chosen primarily for its strong defensive position. However, building the Castle over a cemetery and enclosing the Anglo-Saxon church inside the walls would also have been a statement of power.

This first Castle was built of earth and timber, probably a **motte-and-bailey** castle. Archaeological evidence has been found for the ditch surrounding the wooden wall, but nothing remains of the wooden structures.

This Castle remained in use for almost one-hundred years. In 1095 William II (1087-1100) laid siege to it after it was held against him by the rebel Earl of Northumberland, and during the civil wars, which racked England between 1135 and 1154, it fell into the hands of King David I of Scotland.

Below:
The Norman Castle.

Above: How Curthose's 'New Castle' might have looked.

THE CASTLE AT ITS HEIGHT

In 1154, Henry II came to the throne and set about restoring order after the civil war between his mother Matilda and King Stephen. He took control of Northumberland and Cumbria back from the Scots, and, to secure the border, rebuilt many wooden castles in stone.

Between 1168 and 1178 the wooden Castle was rebuilt by Maurice the Engineer, who also designed Henry's castle at Dover. This was a huge, expensive project, costing £1,144 for a stone **curtain wall** surrounding the Castle, two main gates (the North Gate and Bailey Gate on the west), two **postern** gates (the South and East Posterns) and the **magna turris** or 'great tower', now known as the Keep. The Keep was designed to be a final refuge if the Castle was attacked, an imposing royal residence and a centre of royal administration.

A number of Northumbrian barons were called upon to send knights to garrison the Castle. These barons were also required to build and maintain houses (effectively barracks) within the walls. These were often reported as being in poor repair, as their upkeep was never a popular duty.

Above: A cutaway illustration of the Keep, circa 1200.

Below: The stone Castle, circa 1300.

7

Building continued into the 1200s. By 1216 a separate building called the Great Hall was built by King John which included a kitchen, buttery (for wine butts), pantry and a royal bed-chamber as well as a long aisled feasting hall (see page 24).

The last addition was a **barbican** added to the earlier North Gate. This was ordered by Henry III and built between 1247 and 1250, and is known today as the Black Gate. This created a narrow, angled main entrance passage, defended by gates, towers, a **portcullis** and **turning bridges**.

The Castle became a major mustering point for English armies on their way to campaign in Scotland or to defend against invasions. Edward III (1312-1377) came to Newcastle at least five times on his way to Scotland and his wife Philippa mustered an army here, which defeated the Scots at Neville's Cross near Durham in 1346.

On a day-to-day basis, it was used by the Sheriff of Northumberland as the centre for administering justice and collecting taxes for Northumberland. As such it had two purpose-built prisons (see page 12).

By the late 1200s, Newcastle was an important trading centre. The **Corporation** of Newcastle began to surround the town with a defensive ditch and walls (i.e. the Town Walls), which were completed around 1350. The Castle was no longer the town's sole defence and began to fall into disrepair.

Above: How the barbican may have looked in 1250, and the Black Gate in the present day.

STATE OF DECAY

By the 1500s the Castle was described as 'old and ruinous' – the moat was a **midden**: a dump for the townspeople, and in the 1600s a dunghill was so large that it caused a section of curtain wall to collapse! The basement of the Keep was used as a gaol for the County of Northumberland, with a gaoler's house over the South Postern. The Castle was still a royal fortress and so lay beyond the Corporation's control. This special status made it a haven for 'disorderly persons' – criminals, or those who would not conform with the town's regulations.

In 1618, the Castle was leased by James I to one of his courtiers, Alexander Stephenson, who allowed people to build shops and houses, and charged them rent. During the English Civil War (1642-1651), the Mayor of Newcastle, Sir John Marley, refortified the Castle with artillery **bastions** and cannon.

After the Civil War, the lease holders encouraged private developments and the **Castle Garth** quickly became a bustling community filled with houses, shops and taverns. The Chapel in the Keep was used as a beer cellar, and a garden used for growing vegetables was on top of the Keep walls.

Between 1810 and 1850 many of these houses and shops were demolished to make way for the new Moot Hall courthouse and the railway viaduct. This cleared the area around the Keep and allowed the ruins of the medieval Castle to be appreciated as an historic monument for the first time.

Below: The Castle Garth in the 1700s. Note the vegetable garden on the roof of the Keep.

A JOURNEY THROUGH THE CASTLE
THE BLACK GATE

Principally dating to 1247-50, the building now known as the Black Gate was the last addition to the Castle defences. It was part of a projecting gateway or barbican, designed to keep out invaders and unwanted visitors.

Approaching the gatehouse, you would first have to cross a turning bridge, which spanned the moat. (A turning bridge is a type of drawbridge which is operated by a winch and counterweights.) This approach would have been protected by archers and crossbowmen. The gatehouse was built at an angle to the rest of the walls to provide a better position of defence.

The next obstacle would be a portcullis which could be raised or lowered quickly using ropes or chains. The vertical grooves can still be partially seen today and would originally have extended all the way to the ground.

The rooms on either side of the passage are thought to have been guardrooms and feature arrowslits in their walls for delivering defensive shots. The guards here may also have been the ones responsible for opening a series of double doors or **yetts**, once the person had passed under the portcullis.

A second turning bridge in front of the earlier North Gate would have to be crossed before the visitor could proceed to the rest of the Castle.

Above (top): The building in the early 1800s, surrounded by second-hand clothes shops.

LATER USES

Nobody knows how tall the gatehouse originally was. The second and third floors were added by Alexander Stephenson, who leased the building from James I in 1618 and converted it into lodgings. He owed money to a merchant called Patrick Black and lost the lease on the gatehouse to him when he failed to pay his debt. It is from Patrick Black that the building took its present name.

Below: The Black Gate in a dilapidated state, prior to its 1883-85 restoration.

Over the next two hundred years, the Black Gate deteriorated into a slum, housing up to sixty people at one time. One of the guard-rooms also formed part of the Two Bulls' Heads public house.

At an 1856 council meeting, it was suggested the building was 'a great nuisance' and 'the sooner it was demolished the better'. The Society of Antiquaries of Newcastle upon Tyne lobbied to save it and, eventually, a lease was granted. This included a clause forbidding any part of the building be used as 'an inn, Ale House, or Spirit Shop'.

The Black Gate was restored (see page 26) and served as the Society's archaeological museum until 1960, their Bagpipe Museum until 1987, and their library and offices until 2009.

STRUCK BY PLAGUE

In 1636 a devastating plague killed more than 5,000 people in Newcastle – almost half of the town's population. John Pickells managed a tavern inside the Black Gate at this time. His name and the year '1636' have been found scratched high up on the south west wall, beneath a window. He was perhaps quarantined – locked in the buildings by the authorities to prevent the spread of plague. He was one of the lucky ones; we know from records that John Pickells survived.

Left: Plague doctors wore masks with bird-like beaks because they believed it protected them from the disease.

11

THE CASTLE GARTH

In medieval times, the entire Castle was encircled by a curtain wall, which would have stretched all the way from the North Gate to the South Postern Gate and back around on the east side (see page 25). The yard inside the walls of a castle would usually be known as the bailey. However, the one in Newcastle became known as the Castle Garth – 'garth' being an old word for 'yard'.

Entering via the Black Gate, the visitor would then have passed two prisons: the Great Pit, which was in one of the towers of the earlier North gate, and the Heron Pit. These dark prisons were used to hold common criminals and their upkeep was evidently not of high priority. In 1357 the ceiling of the Great Pit collapsed, almost killing those incarcerated, due to 'rotting of the joists'.

Below:
The Castle Garth, looking toward the Black Gate, circa 1900. The Heron Pit was hidden beneath later buildings until 1905.

In 1905, W. H. Knowles excavated the Heron Pit. He discovered holes in the walls, designed for holding massive beams to support the floor above. A trapdoor, secured by an iron bar, would have provided the only access to what was 'a prison of great depth, without the provision of light or air in the four-square walls' (BREEZE).

Above the pit can be seen the remains of a medieval **garderobe**. The fireplace and chimney appear to have been part of the later housing built here.

HAMMER OF THE POOR

The Heron Pit is named after William Heron, Sheriff of Northumberland from 1247 until his death in 1257. He was known for cruelly profiteering from taxes and holding citizens for unjust ransoms in the pit. A year after he died, he was described as 'the greediest of men', the 'hammer of the poor and persecutor of the religious', bringing to mind the infamous Sheriff of Nottingham in the Robin Hood legends.

Above: The Heron Pit today.

The primary chamber in the basement of the Keep is popularly referred to as the Garrison Room, although there is no evidence that soldiers were garrisoned here; in reality it was probably used for storage. Its longest usage was as a gaol, from the Tudor period (1485-1603) to the early 1800s.

During this period, regular court sessions called **assizes** took place in the building known as the Moot Hall (formerly the Great Hall; see page 24). The gaol was used to hold prisoners whilst they awaited their trials.

In 1787, prison reformer John Howard wrote: 'The county prisoners are men and women, confined together seven or eight nights, in a dirty damp dungeon, six steps in the old castle, which, having no roof, in wet season the water is some inches deep'. The metal rings where prisoners were chained can still be seen on the walls and central pillar.

The remains of a lead pipe can be seen on the column in the centre of the room. Through this, water was carried from the Well Room on the third floor, forming part of a medieval plumbing system.

The largest of two flights of stairs leads to a small chamber which is now called the Pit Room. Its original purpose is unknown but suggestions include a second store room or a prison cell. In the late 1700s the floor was dug out to become an ice house.

The Pit Room is believed by some to have been a condemned cell, for prisoners who had been tried and were awaiting death by execution.

HANGED, DRAWN AND QUARTERED

Father and son William and Humphrey Lisle were two notable prisoners who were locked up for their criminal activities. They escaped the gaol and wreaked havoc, pillaging towns and villages with a crew of fellow outlaws. Upon their re-capture in 1528, William, the father, was '**hanged, drawn and quartered**'. Humphrey, the youngest at only 12 or 13 years old, was allowed to live.

TOWN AND COUNTY

The town of Newcastle became separate from the County of Northumberland in 1400, however the Castle – being property of the King – was not included. This meant that despite having given the town its name, it remained part of Northumberland, and not part of Newcastle at all. This is why the assizes were held here on behalf of the County of Northumberland.

AIR-RAID SHELTER

The gaol stopped being used as such in the early 1800s. During World War II the room served as a public air-raid shelter. The east doorway, leading to the Mezzanine Chamber, was sealed by a brick wall which remained in place until 2013. The door at street level had its frame painted white to guide people in the dark.

A second air-raid shelter was built just north of the Black Gate and part of it is still in use as an electricity substation. A colourful mural, painted on it in 2014, depicts people and objects from Newcastle's past.

Another room, the Mezzanine Chamber, is today accessible via a small flight of stairs in the east wall. Its original purpose remains a mystery.

Perhaps the most remarkable room in the Keep is the Chapel; its vaulted ceiling and zig-zag patterned arches are quintessentially Norman. There would have been a second chapel in the grounds of the Castle for the garrison to use. The Chapel in the Keep was probably reserved for royalty, officers of the garrisons and important guests.

The doorway leading from the Chapel into the small 'ante-chamber' and into the rest of the Keep is a later addition, although it cannot be accurately dated. Originally the Chapel was kept separate from the rest of the Keep to prevent it being used by attackers as an easy point of access.

Above: The room in two of its various guises: as a 'dirty, damp dungeon' (left) and displaying artifacts from the Society of Antiquaries' collection (right). Bottom: A surviving metal ring which was used to hold prisoners' chains.

The stone object on display in the **nave** is a 'piscina' or water basin, while the hole set into the wall of the chancel is the aumbry – the cupboard where the chalice, bread and wine were kept for the ceremony of the Eucharist.

By the 1780s, the Chapel had become a beer cellar for the neighbouring Three Bulls' Heads public house (not to be mistaken with the Two Bulls' Heads at the Black Gate). This was one of the buildings demolished to make way for the railway. Famed Tyneside architect John Dobson was employed from 1847-8 to replace crumbling stonework and restore its former grandeur.

Above: A torchlit tour of the Chapel, prior to restoration.

ST NICHOLAS CATHEDRAL

St Nicholas Cathedral is located nearby. Still a working church, its gothic architecture, including the extravagant Lantern Tower, dates primarily to the 1440s.

A parish church is thought to have stood on this site since the 1090s, around a decade after the founding of Curthose's wooden Castle, and may have replaced an earlier parish church which was enclosed within the walls of the Castle.

It became a cathedral in 1882, when Newcastle was elevated from being a town to a city.

Left: The Chapel.

SAVIOURS OF THE CASTLE

The Society of Antiquaries of Newcastle upon Tyne (SANT) is the oldest and largest provincial antiquarian society in the country.

Formed in 1813, they held their meetings in the Keep until 1819. In 1847 they took a lease of the entire building and in 1848 a 'subscription banquet' was held in the Great Hall to raise money.

The Society later saved and carried out a major restoration of the Black Gate (1883-85), opening it as a museum for their various artifacts.

In 2009 the Society moved from the Black Gate to The Great North Museum: Hancock. They are still very much involved with managing the site.

Above: SANT's emblem.

The main room on the first floor is the Lower Hall, which may have been the station of the **Constable** who would oversee activity in the Castle. Much of the Lower Hall's appearance, including the fireplace, chimney breast and central pillar, comes from the 1810-12 restoration.

During the restoration, part of the wall of the Lower Hall was removed to allow access to what is now the reception kiosk of the Keep. Another addition at this time was the current wooden door onto the external staircase.

In the 1820s, this room was used as a prison for female debtors, then afterwards as a classroom for Sunday school pupils until approximately 1848. The room was used as a library and reading room for the Society of Antiquaries, until they relocated to the Black Gate in the 1880s, moving their collection with them.

A room on the north of the Lower Hall is a **solar**. It would have served one of the officers of the Castle as a bedroom, office and meeting room. This self-contained suite was a comfortable one, as can be seen from the fact it has its own fireplace and a garderobe just around the corner.

This room is popularly known as the Queen's Chamber; however, there is no record of royalty having stayed here. Many of the rooms in the Keep were given romantic names in the 1800s, which have stuck over time despite their lack of historical basis.

Above: The Lower Hall circa early 1880s, prior to the library being relocated to the Black Gate.

THE WORST JOB IN THE CASTLE

In the Keep, there are several seats with large circular holes; these are garderobes (medieval toilets). Waste would fall down a chute within the wall; then it was somebody's unpleasant job to clear it. A small doorway (pictured above) can be seen at street level, on the western side of the Keep, and would have led to one of these compartments.

Above: The Lower Hall today.

Above: The Queen's Chamber.

Above: The Lower Hall today.

SECOND FLOOR

The principal room in the Keep is known as the Great Hall, however this is another romantic Victorian name. (The actual Great Hall was elsewhere on the Castle Garth and was a separate building; see page 24.) Nevertheless, this room probably would have been used for meetings, audiences and other grand occasions.

The ceiling is a brick arch inserted between 1810-12. Previously, the Keep had been roofless for centuries. Two sets of beam holes can be seen in the walls: the higher of the two belongs to the original ceiling and roof structure. It has been speculated that the lower set of holes may be from the Civil War, when soldiers are said to have constructed a temporary timber ceiling.

The room may originally have been heated by braziers; the chimney breast is a much later addition. The fireplace, dated 1599, came from an inn on Sandhill and was part of the 1810-12 restoration.

Up a flight of stairs in the Great Hall, secreted away in the north wall, is a room which was used as a cell for prisoners. We can tell this by the holes outside, which would have housed a heavy bar to lock the door.

It would have been a fairly comfortable room, with its own private garderobe, and so would have housed knights and other important prisoners, usually kept for political reasons.

On the northeast side of the Hall is the Well Room. When the well was cleaned out in the early 1900s, it was found to be 99 feet (over 30m) deep. If the Castle was besieged, the clean water supply was essential.

On either side of the well are basins which distributed water via lead pipes down to the lower levels of the Keep (see page 13). The holes on the wall above the well show where the **windlass** used to be.

THE CAPTURED PRINCESS

Mary Bruce, the sister of Scottish king Robert the Bruce, was imprisoned in the Keep between 1310 and 1314. She was moved to Newcastle from Roxburgh where she had already been imprisoned for several years. She was eventually exchanged for English prisoners following her brother's victory at the Battle of Bannockburn.

WE TWO KINGS

Christmas 1292 saw an historic meeting take place at the Castle. On 26 December, John Balliol, the King of Scotland, paid homage to Edward I of England. This act of fealty gave England the upper hand over Scotland and started a period of humiliation for the Scots.

In 1296, a Scottish rebellion was crushed at the Battle of Dunbar. In 1297 the tables turned when Sir William Wallace (famously portrayed by Mel Gibson in the film *Braveheart*) and Sir Andrew Moray raised a rebellion which defeated the English at Stirling Bridge and raided northern England as far as York, though their lack of siege equipment meant that Newcastle remained a safe haven for refugees.

When Wallace was captured and executed by King Edward I in 1305, his body was quartered and his right arm sent to Newcastle, to be displayed on the medieval Tyne Bridge (Bruce).

Opposite page: The Great Hall.
Above right: John Balliol before King Edward I © Bibliotèque municipale de Besançon.

A door in the south-west corner of the Great Hall leads to an apartment now known as the King's Chamber, very similar in layout to the Queen's Chamber. This is another solar, with its own garderobe.

Due to its proximity to the Great Hall, it is likely that this was used by the most important guests. The fireplace dates to the Keep's construction and is one of the earliest in Britain to remain in its original state.

On the opposite wall, two names – John Danby and Thomas Cuthbert, along with the year 1644 – can be seen carved into the stone. These likely date from the Siege of Newcastle during the English Civil War, during which the Castle was refortified.

Above: The King's Chamber fireplace (top), and an illustration by Robert Bertram, from 'The Walls of Newcastle upon Tyne', 1951.

SIEGE AND STORM

From August to October 1644, a Scottish army allied with Parliament besieged Newcastle. (A Scottish chronicler reported: *'the enemy from the castle doth mightily annoy us with their great artillery'.*)

The Town Walls were breached on 19 October and the Scots entered Newcastle. Mayor John Marley and his troops held out at the Castle for three more days before finally surrendering.

The Scots occupied Newcastle until January 1647.

Above: A reeanactment was held at the Castle in October 2014 to mark 370 years since the Siege

THE ROOF

The paved flat roof, along with its crenelated **parapets** and corner turrets, only dates from 1810-12. The Corporation of Newcastle purchased the Keep for £630, and Alderman Forster spearheaded the restoration.

A 'noon gun' was fired regularly until the 1850s when – after a number of accidents, in one of which a gunner was killed – the practice was discontinued. The twelve cannon (old naval carronades) remained until the 1930s.

The battlements reflected the gothic fashions of the time, and also the medieval romances made popular by the novels of Sir Walter Scott. The work received some criticism for being 'quite out of character with the architecture of the Keep' (CHARLETON). Today these battlements give the Keep its distinctive outline and the roof boasts spectacular 360° views across the city and the Newcastle and Gateshead Quayside.

ROLL UP, ROLL UP...

A number of entertainers have performed spectacular stunts atop the Keep. In 1733 a donkey was 'flown' from the building – however, catastrophe struck and the donkey plummeted to the ground, killing a young girl, according to contemporary reports.

Harry Houdini, the world-famous escapologist, performed stunts in 1920, dangling precariously above the street below.

Above: An archer takes aim from the roof of the Keep.

Inset: A view of the Tyne Bridge and the Swing Bridge from the Keep, August 1963. © Tyne & Wear Archives and Museums.

GALLERIES AND STAIRS

Flights of spiral stairs give access to two narrow galleries which encircle the Keep, running inside the thickness of the walls. Arrowslits are present on all four sides, through which the Castle could be defended by archers.

Originally the upper gallery would have looked out onto the pitched wooden roof of the Keep. There may have been a wooden floored attic accessible here for maintenance.

On the lower gallery is a staircase which has either been blocked off deliberately or never finished. This is known as the Unfinished Stairs and might date to 1173 when King William the Lion of Scotland invaded northern England, possibly interrupting work on the Keep.

MASONS' MARKS

In this gallery, and throughout the Keep, strange angular marks can be seen carved into the stone. These are masons' marks, which were carved by the craftsmen who originally built the Keep. Their exact purpose is unknown, but the most popular theory is that each mark relates to a specific mason, who would mark his work when finished so that the Master Mason could ensure payment for the amount of work done.

JOHN DOBSON

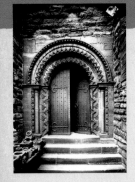

The extravagant outer doorway to the Great Hall was repaired by Victorian architect John Dobson who also designed Newcastle's Grey Street and Central Station. The decoration here and in the Chapel (see page 15) had greatly deteriorated; however, fortunately Dobson had created sketches as a young man when it was in a more intact state, which helped guide his restoration. At the head of the **forebuilding** stairs is a room believed to have been a small private chapel, which was also extensively reworked by Dobson.

Left: Doorway to the Great Hall.

COMING OF THE RAILWAYS

With the construction of the railway viaduct in the 1840s, the Black Gate and Keep were cut off from one another. The lower town, the Quayside and the Close, became isolated from the rapidly developing town centre.

Newcastle played a significant role in the Industrial Revolution; George Stephenson's *Rocket*, one of the world's first steam locomotives, was engineered a short distance from the Castle. The Keep was briefly threatened with demolition during the construction of the railway; however, prominent historian John Collingwood Bruce was determined that it should not be destroyed. The Society of Antiquaries took a lease on the building a short time afterwards.

The viaduct thankfully just avoids the Keep. The railway's impact on the Garth was dramatic, nonetheless. All buildings immediately surrounding the Keep were demolished at that time.

When the Black Gate came under threat a decade later, advocates for its demolition called it a 'barbarous relic of antiquity'. The former gatehouse had become 'lost' behind later buildings for nearly two hundred years. It was perhaps only reprieved by the fact slum housing had been cleared to make way for the railway.

Below: Newcastle's complex 'Diamond Crossing' was once the largest railway crossing in the world.

WHAT IS MISSING?

THE (GREATER) GREAT HALL

Above: 'View of the Old Castle of Newcastle upon Tyne', circa 1780.

The Castle Garth would have been a bustling place filled with buildings which are now lost. Perhaps the most unfortunate loss is the Old Moot Hall – which was originally the Great Hall of the Castle. It stood where the Vermont Hotel and the courtyard of the present Moot Hall courthouse is today.

This building was much larger than the hall in the Keep and had 'a nave and aisles with circular piers' (Pevsner & Richmond). There also would have been a kitchen where hot food could be prepared, as well as other domestic buildings.

When it held assizes from Tudor times onwards, prisoners were tried in this building after being transferred from the Castle's gaol (see page 13). Between assize sessions, the Moot Hall was a cultural venue – it seems to have been used as a theatre as early as 1711, and plays were performed here until Newcastle's first Theatre Royal opened in Mosley Street in 1788. In 1751 a dancing school was also held here. Both were popular pastimes for Georgian society. It was demolished in 1810 and replaced by the present purpose-built Moot Hall.

Above: Detail from a 1545 plan of Newcastle, showing the Queen's Mantle on the right.

THE QUEEN'S MANTLE

The Queen's Mantle was a round defensive tower which stood on the hilltop now occupied by the Moot Hall. It had various rooms and it has been speculated it had a platform for guards and contained a kitchen and pantry.

During the Civil War it was redeveloped and fortified with artillery and became known as the Half Moon **Battery**, to reflect its new usage. The Siege of Newcastle in 1644 marked the final time the Castle was utilised to defend the town.

WALLS AND BOUNDARIES

Substantial parts of the south curtain wall survive above ground between the Keep and the Close (i.e. next to the riverfront). The remains of a tower stand behind the Bridge Hotel pub, which continues a long tradition of public houses in the Garth. The most famous was the Three Bulls' Heads, which stood approximately ten metres north of the Keep. The earliest mention is from 1709, and it was demolished in 1847. It was a focal point for the local community; when a new tradesman wanted to set up business in the Garth, a meeting of established traders was held here to approve the newcomer.

Much of the south curtain wall, including a well, was excavated between 1966 and 1970, and conserved thereafter by Newcastle City Council. The impressive South Postern Gate stands near the top of Castle Stairs. The east curtain wall and remains of the East Postern were uncovered in the 1980s, at the head of Dog Leap Stairs.

Above: Castle Stairs, circa 1904. Below: The South Postern Gate.

This part of the Castle Garth, extending to the Black Gate, was once renowned as 'the town's emporium of discarded finery' (WELFORD). Shoemakers, cobblers, tailors and second-hand clothes shops traded here from the 1600s onwards. The Garth was outside the jurisdiction of the town so traders and craftsmen could operate free of the guild restrictions. This was good news for 'undesirables' at the time, such as **Dissenters** and Scotsmen, who were not allowed to open businesses elsewhere in the town.

RESTORATIONS AND CURRENT USE

The first major restoration of the Keep took place between 1810 and 1812, led by the Corporation of Newcastle. Later, in the 1840s, the Society of Antiquaries carried out further restorations under the supervision of architect John Dobson. Between the 1960s and 1980s, crumbling stonework was replaced, the interior cleaned and the Society's collections cleared out.

The Black Gate was restored by the Society between 1883 and 1885. The rooms were modernised and a new external flight of stairs added, designed by architect and Society member R.J. Johnson. The top floor became a flat for the warden of the Keep and the present red-pantiled roof was added.

In 2011 a Heritage Lottery Fund grant was awarded to bring the Black Gate back into public use. A lift was added in 2013 and new interpretation installed. 'Newcastle Castle' opened in March 2015, reuniting the Keep and Black Gate for the first time in over 160 years. It is managed by The Heart of the City Partnership – made up of representatives from Newcastle City Council, St Nicholas Cathedral and The Society of Antiquaries of Newcastle upon Tyne, as well as selected independent members of the regional business community.

Below:
The Keep, circa 1840s.

Above: The Black Gate, 1883.

Above: The Black Gate, circa 1890, shortly after opening as a museum.
Below: Renovation of the Black Gate, 2013.

ove: The Keep, pictured from roughly the same position, during and after its 1810-12 restoration.

27

HISTORY TIMELINE

122 Hadrian's Wall begun

43 AD Roman invasion of Britain

500-600 Anglo-Saxon kingdoms develop

c.410 End of Roman rule in Britain

1066 Norman invasion of England

793 Vikings sack Lindisfarne

1296-1603 Invasion of Scotland by Edward I begins over 300 years of intermittent warfare

1455-1487 The War of the Roses

1347-1349 The Black Death

c. 200 Fort of Pons Aelius built in stone

c. 400 Fort of Pons Aelius abandoned with the end of Roman rule in Britain

c. 700 Site of Pons Aelius becomes an Anglo-Saxon cemetery

1080 The 'New Castle' founded

1139-1157 Newcastle falls into Scottish hands

1168-1178 The Castle is rebuilt in stone

1247-1250 Black Gate added to the Castle

1248 The first Tyne Bridge is built on the site of the present-day Swing Bridge

1260-1279 Construction of the Town Walls begins

1292 John Balliol pays homage to Edward I at the Castle

1310-1314 Mary Bruce imprisoned in the Castle

158 During the reig of Elizabeth I th Castle is describe as 'old and ruinou

Below: A painting by Victorian artist John Storey, recreating Newcastle as it appeared in approximately 1600.

1603
'Union of the
>wns' (James VI of
;cotland becomes
mes I of England)

1642-1651
English Civil Wars

1715 & 1745
Jacobite
Rebellions

1815
Battle of Waterloo

1837-1901
Queen Victoria reigns.
Revolutions in Europe

1914-1918
World War I

1939-1945
World War II

1636
utbreak of plague
kills nearly half
the population
of Newcastle

1644
The refortified
Castle is used to
defend the town
during the Siege
of Newcastle

1646
Charles I held
prisoner in
Newcastle

1771
In November
flooding hits
Newcastle.
The Great
Flood washes
away the
medieval
Tyne Bridge

1810-1812
Newcastle Corporation
purchases the Keep and
begin restoration

1835-1839
Development of
modern Newcastle by
Richard Grainger and
John Dobson

1847-1848
John Dobson carries out
restoration work to the Keep

1854
The Great Fire of Gateshead
& Newcastle kills 53
people and wipes out a
swathe of buildings on
both sides of the river

1928
Tyne Bridge
opened

1939-1945
The Keep is
used is used
as an air raid
shelter during
World War II

1960-1992
Archaeological
excavations in
the Castle Garth

1876
Swing Bridge built

1882
Newcastle becomes a city and
St Nicholas becomes a cathedral

2001
Millennium
Bridge opened

2015
Black Gate
reopens
following
Heritage
Lottery-funded
renovations

APPENDIX

GLOSSARY

Assizes A former court held at regular intervals in each county in England and Wales until the 1970s.

Barbican The outer defences of a castle, particularly a gate or drawbridge.

Bastion A fortification to take artillery, usually of triangular plan.

Battery A fortified emplacement for heavy guns or cannon.

Castle Garth The area within the castle walls, 'garth' being an old term for 'yard'.

Constable The person in charge of a castle when the owner was not in residence.

Corporation The governing body of the town, consisting of an elected mayor and a number of burgesses or property-owners.

Curtain Wall The area wall which enclosed the defended area of a stone-built castle.

Dissenter A member of any Protestant group which was not within the Church of England e.g. Quakers and Anabaptists.

Forebuilding A defensible structure containing a gateway on the entrance stair.

Garderobe A medieval toilet. Garderobes were often used to store clothes as it was believed that the smell would stop moths from eating them.

Hanged, drawn and quartered A punishment in which the person was hung by the neck until semi-conscious and dismembered, used for Englishmen found guilty of high treason.

Magna turris 'Great Tower.' The term used to describe the Keep in early chronicles.

Midden A heap of rubbish or a dunghill.

Motte-and-bailey A high mound (motte) of earth with a timber, or occasionally stone, tower on top, and with an attached earth-banked enclosure (bailey) topped with a wooden palisade.

Nave The central part of a church or hall.

Parapet A low wall on the outside of the walkway along the top of a curtain wall or tower, often with crenellations.

Postern An entrance at the back or side of a castle.

Portcullis A wooden grille sliding vertically in grooves cut in stone either side of a gateway.

Solar A private chamber.

Turning Bridge A counterweighted bridge on a central pivot.

Windlass A type of winch, used here to lower and raise water from a well.

Yetts Wrought iron gate or grille. Like a portcullis, but hinged like a gate rather than raised and lowered.

BIBLIOGRAPHY

Breeze, David J. (ed.), *The Society of Antiquaries of Newcastle Upon Tyne 1813-2013* (Newcastle upon Tyne: Statex Colour Print, 2013), p.49

Bruce, John C., *A Hand-book to Newcastle-on-Tyne* (Newcastle upon Tyne, 1863), p.74

Charleton, R.J., *The Monthly chronicle of North-country lore and legend* (May 1887), p.122

Howard, John, *The State of the Prisons in England and Wales: Volume 1* (Warrington, William Eyres, 1777), p.425

Pesvner, Nikolaus & Richmond, Ian, *The Buildings of England, Northumberland* (Middlesex: Penguin, 1957; revised and reprinted in 1992), p. 235

Speed, John, *The history of Great Britaine under the conquests of ye Romans, Saxons, Danes and Normans* (London, 1614), p. 421

Welford, Richard et al., *Northumbrian History, Literature, and Art* (Newcastle upon Tyne: Andrew Reid & Company Ltd., 1898), p.207

RECOMMENDED READING

Bath, Jo and Stevenson, Richard F., *The Newcastle Book of Days* (Gloucestershire: The History Press, 2013)

Collingwood Bruce, John, *A Guide to the Castle of Newcastle upon Tyne*, illustrated with plans, etc. (London: Hamilton, Adams and co., 1847)

Ellwood, Steve, *Newcastle in 50 Buildings* (Gloucester: Amberley Publishing, 2016)

Graham, Frank, *Newcastle: A Short History and Guide* (Northumberland: Butler Publishing, 1988)

Grundy, John, *John Grundy's History of Newcastle* (Newcastle upon Tyne: Tyne Bridge Publishing, 2016)

Hutchinson, Ken, *Lost Newcastle in Colour* (Gloucester: Amberley Publishing, 2014)

Longstaffe, *Archaeologia Aeliana: The New Castle upon Tyne* (New series, Vol.4. 1860)

Mackenzie, E., *A Descriptive and Historical Account of the Town and County of Newcastle and the Borough of Gateshead* (Newcastle upon Tyne: Mackenzie and Dent, 1827)

Morton, Dave, *Newcastle in the Headlines* (Gloucester: Amberley Publishing, 2015)

Nolan, John, *The Castle of Newcastle upon Tyne after c.1600*, (Fifth Series, Vol.18.1990)

Sadler, John and Serdiville, Rosie, *The Great Siege of Newcastle 1644* (Gloucestershire: The History Press, 2011)

Smith, Ken and Yellowley, Tom, *The Great Walls of Newcastle: Exploring the City's Ancient Defences* (Newcastle: Tyne Bridge Publishing, 2012)

Terry, C.S, *The Siege of Newcastle-upon-Tyne by the Scots in 1644* (Arch. Ael. Second Series, Vol.21, 1889)

THE KEEP FLOORPLANS

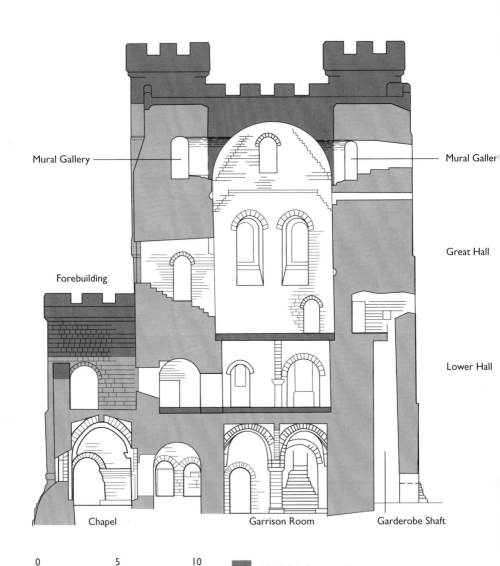

Mural Gallery

Mural Galler

Great Hall

Forebuilding

Lower Hall

Chapel

Garrison Room

Garderobe Shaft

0   5   10

metres

19th/20th Century alterations